SPENCER BLAKE

Be an Entrepreneur

How to become the best CEO ever

Introduction

How to Become the Best CEO Ever

Becoming the best CEO is an aspiration that requires a blend of vision, leadership, strategic thinking, and a deep understanding of both the organization and the market in which it operates. It involves mastering a diverse set of skills, cultivating a visionary mindset, and demonstrating unwavering commitment to excellence. Whether you're steering an established organization or launching a new venture, the principles of effective leadership and entrepreneurial success are foundational to achieving remarkable results.

The Path Forward

This introduction sets the stage for a deeper exploration into each of these areas, providing practical insights and strategies to help you become the best CEO and entrepreneur. Whether you're at the helm of a growing startup or leading an established company, these principles will guide you in navigating the complexities of business leadership and entrepreneurship, driving your organization towards sustained success and making a lasting impact in your industry. This book is a comprehensive guide on how to achieve this lofty goal.

Chapter 1

Develop a Clear Vision

Understand Your Industry

To lead effectively, you must possess a deep understanding of the industry. Stay informed about trends, competitors, and emerging technologies.

Define Your Mission

Craft a clear, compelling mission statement that reflects the core values and objectives of your organization. This mission should inspire and guide every decision and action taken by your company.

Defining your mission is a critical step in setting the foundation for your leadership as a CEO. Here's how you can effectively define your mission:

1. Understand Your Core Purpose

Identify Your Why

Reflect on why your organization exists beyond making a profit. Consider what drives your company's operations and what impact you aim to make in the world.

Focus on Your Core Values

Determine the fundamental principles and beliefs that guide your organization's behavior and decision-making. These values should be central to your mission.

2. Consider Your Stakeholders

Employees

Think about what inspires and motivates your employees. A compelling mission should resonate with them and provide a sense of purpose in their work.

Customers

Understand the needs and aspirations of your customers. Your mission should reflect how your company seeks to meet these needs and deliver value to them.

Community

Consider the broader community and the role your organization plays within it. Your mission can highlight your commitment to social responsibility and positive impact.

3. Articulate Your Goals

Long-term Vision

Your mission should provide a glimpse of your long-term vision for the organization. It should set the direction for where you want the company to go.

Achievable Objectives

While your mission should be ambitious, it should also be realistic and attainable. Set clear objectives that guide your organization's efforts and strategies.

4. Crafting the Mission Statement

Keep It Simple

A mission statement should be concise and easy to understand. Avoid jargon and complex language. Aim for a statement that is memorable and easily communicated.

Be Specific

While brevity is important, ensure your mission statement is specific enough to provide clear guidance. It should give a precise sense of what your organization aims to achieve.

Inspire and Motivate

Your mission should inspire and motivate everyone connected to the organization. It should evoke a sense of pride and commitment among employees and stakeholders.

5. Review and Refine

Seek Feedback

Once you have a draft, seek feedback from key stakeholders including employees, board members, and trusted advisors. Their insights can help refine the statement.

Revise as Needed

Be open to making revisions based on the feedback you receive. The mission statement should evolve until it perfectly encapsulates your organization's core purpose and direction.

Communicate and Embed

Once finalized, communicate your mission statement clearly and consistently. Embed it into your company's culture, ensuring that it guides daily operations, decision-making, and strategic planning.

Example Mission Statements

Google: "To organize the world's information and make it universally accessible and useful."

Tesla: "To accelerate the world's transition to sustainable energy."

Patagonia: "We're in business to save our home planet."

These examples illustrate how a well-defined mission statement succinctly conveys the purpose, values, and overarching goals of an organization.

Defining your mission is more than just a formality; it is the cornerstone of your leadership strategy. A clear, compelling mission statement aligns your organization's efforts, motivates your team, and communicates your purpose to the world. By carefully crafting and consistently living by your mission, you lay the groundwork for achieving lasting success as a CEO.

Set Long-term Goals

Establish long-term goals that are ambitious yet achievable. These should align with your mission and drive the company towards its vision.

Setting long-term goals is a vital aspect of effective leadership and strategic planning. These goals provide direction, motivate your team, and help measure progress over time. Here's a detailed guide on how to set meaningful long-term goals:

1. Align with Vision and Mission

Reflect on Your Mission

Ensure that your long-term goals are aligned with the mission statement of your organization. Your goals should help advance your mission and contribute to achieving your overall vision.

Consider the Vision

Long-term goals should be stepping stones toward realizing your vision.

They should reflect the future state you want your organization to achieve.

2. Conduct a SWOT Analysis

Strengths

Identify the strengths of your organization that can be leveraged to achieve your long-term goals. Consider core competencies, resources, and capabilities.

Weaknesses

Acknowledge areas where the organization may need improvement or face challenges. Setting goals to address these weaknesses can be crucial for long-term success.

Opportunities

Look for external opportunities in the market, such as emerging trends, technological advancements, and market gaps that your organization can capitalize on.

Threats

Be aware of potential threats such as competition, market changes, and regulatory challenges. Set goals to mitigate these risks.

3. Be Specific and Measurable

Define Clear Objectives

Long-term goals should be specific, detailing what you aim to achieve. Vague goals can lead to confusion and lack of direction.

Establish Measurable Criteria

Set measurable criteria to track progress. Use key performance indicators (KPIs) to quantify your goals, making it easier to monitor achievements and make adjustments as needed.

4. Set Realistic and Achievable Goals

Consider Resources

Ensure your goals are realistic given your current resources, including financial, human, and technological assets. Overly ambitious goals can lead to frustration and demotivation.

Break Down Goals

Divide long-term goals into smaller, manageable milestones. This approach makes it easier to achieve progress and maintain momentum.

5. Time-bound Goals

Set a Timeline

Define a clear timeline for achieving your long-term goals. A time-bound framework creates a sense of urgency and helps in planning and prioritizing tasks.

Review and Adjust

Regularly review your goals and timelines. Be flexible and willing to adjust them based on changing circumstances or new information.

6. Involve Your Team

Collaborative Goal Setting

Engage your team in the goal-setting process. Collaborative goal setting fosters buy-in and ensures that everyone understands and is committed to achieving the goals.

Assign Responsibilities

Clearly define who is responsible for each aspect of achieving the goals. Assigning responsibilities ensures accountability and clarity.

7. Monitor and Evaluate Progress

Regular Check-ins

Schedule regular check-ins to monitor progress toward your long-term goals. These check-ins help identify any issues early and allow for timely interventions.

Measure Success

Use the established KPIs to measure success. Regular evaluation helps in understanding what is working and what needs adjustment.

Celebrate Milestones

Acknowledge and celebrate the achievement of milestones. Recognizing progress keeps the team motivated and focused on the ultimate goal.

8. Adjust as Needed

Be Flexible

Be prepared to adjust your goals as needed. Market conditions, technological changes, and other external factors may require you to pivot or refine your goals.

Learn from Experience

Use the insights gained from monitoring and evaluation to improve your goal-setting process. Learning from successes and failures helps in setting better goals in the future.

Example of Long-term Goals

Increase Market Share: Aim to increase market share by 15% over the next five years through strategic acquisitions and innovative product development.
Sustainability Goals: Commit to reducing the company's carbon footprint by 40% within ten years by implementing green technologies and sustainable

practices.

Global Expansion: Establish a presence in five new international markets within the next decade, focusing on regions with high growth potential.

Setting long-term goals is essential for steering your organization toward sustained success. These goals provide a road map for achieving your vision and fulfilling your mission. By being specific, realistic, and collaborative in your approach, and by regularly monitoring and adjusting your goals, you can ensure that your organization remains focused, motivated, and adaptable in an ever-changing business landscape.

Chapter 2

Build and Lead a Strong Team

Hire the Right People
Surround yourself with talented, motivated individuals who share your vision and values. Look for diversity in skills and perspectives to foster innovation.

Hiring the right people is fundamental to the success of any organization. The right employees not only perform their roles effectively but also contribute to a positive company culture and drive long-term growth. Here's a detailed guide on how to hire the right people:

1. Define the Role Clearly

Create a Detailed Job Description
Clearly outline the responsibilities, qualifications, skills, and experience required for the position. This helps in attracting candidates who are a good fit for the role.

Identify Key Competencies
Determine the essential skills and attributes needed for the job. Consider both technical skills and soft skills such as communication, teamwork, and problem-solving.

2. Develop an Effective Recruitment Strategy

Utilize Multiple Channels

Advertise job openings on various platforms including job boards, social media, company website, and industry-specific sites. This broadens your reach and attracts a diverse pool of candidates.

Employee Referrals

Encourage current employees to refer candidates. Referrals can often lead to high-quality hires as employees typically recommend individuals they believe would be a good fit for the company.

Work with Recruiters

Consider partnering with recruitment agencies, especially for specialized roles. Recruiters can provide access to a larger talent pool and assist with the hiring process.

3. Screen Candidates Effectively

Review Resumes and Applications

Carefully review resumes and cover letters to identify candidates who meet the job requirements. Look for relevant experience, skills, and accomplishments.

Pre-Screening Interviews

Conduct initial phone or video interviews to further assess candidates' qualifications and fit for the role. This helps in narrowing down the pool of applicants before scheduling in-person interviews.

4. Conduct Thorough Interviews

Structured Interviews

Use a structured interview process with standardized questions to ensure consistency and fairness. This helps in objectively comparing candidates.

Behavioral Questions

Ask behavioral questions to understand how candidates have handled situations in the past. This can provide insights into their problem-solving abilities, teamwork, and work ethic.

Technical Assessments

For roles that require specific technical skills, consider conducting technical assessments or practical tests. This helps in evaluating candidates' proficiency in required skills.

5. Assess Cultural Fit

Company Values

Evaluate whether candidates' values align with the company's culture and values. Cultural fit is crucial for long-term employee satisfaction and retention.

Team Dynamics

Consider how candidates will fit within the existing team. Assess their interpersonal skills and ability to collaborate effectively with others.

Soft Skills

Look for soft skills such as adaptability, communication, and emotional intelligence. These skills are essential for thriving in a dynamic work environment.

6. Check References

Professional References

Contact previous employers to verify candidates' work history, performance, and conduct. This provides valuable insights into their reliability and capabilities.

Ask Detailed Questions

Inquire about specific aspects of the candidate's job performance, strengths, areas for improvement, and overall behavior in the workplace.

7. Make an Informed Decision

Compare Candidates

Evaluate all candidates based on their skills, experience, interview performance, and cultural fit. Consider both immediate needs and long-term potential.

Involve Key Stakeholders

Involve relevant team members or department heads in the decision-making process. Their input can provide different perspectives and help in making a well-rounded decision.

Offer and Negotiate

Once you've identified the right candidate, extend a job offer. Be prepared to negotiate terms such as salary, benefits, and start date to reach a mutually agreeable arrangement.

8. Onboard Effectively

Comprehensive On boarding

Provide a structured on boarding program to help new hires acclimate to the company. This should include orientation, training, and introduction to team members and company processes.

Continuous Support

Offer continuous support and check-ins during the initial period. This helps new employees feel welcome, supported, and equipped to succeed in their new role

Hiring the right people is crucial for building a successful and sustainable organization. By defining roles clearly, developing an effective recruitment strategy, conducting thorough interviews, and assessing both skills and cultural fit, you can attract and retain top talent. Remember, the hiring process doesn't end with the job offer; effective on boarding and continuous support are essential for ensuring new hires integrate well and contribute to the company's success.

Foster a Positive Culture

Create a workplace environment that values transparency,inclusiveness, and collaboration. Encourage open communication and recognize achievements.

Fostering a positive culture within your organization is essential for enhancing employee morale, boosting productivity, and ensuring long-term success. A positive workplace culture nurtures a sense of belonging, encourages collaboration, and helps attract and retain top talent. Here's how to foster such a culture:

1. Define and Communicate Core Values

Establish Core Values

Identify the fundamental principles that reflect your organization's beliefs and priorities. Core values should guide behavior and decision-making within the company.

Communicate Consistently

Ensure these values are clearly communicated to all employees. Incorporate them into on boarding processes, training programs, and everyday interactions.

2. Lead by Example

Model Desired Behavior

Leaders should exemplify the behaviors and attitudes they wish to see in their employees. Demonstrating integrity, respect, and enthusiasm sets a positive tone for the organization.

Be Accessible

Maintain an open-door policy. Encourage employees to share ideas, ask questions, and express concerns. Approach-ability builds trust and openness.

3. Promote Work-Life Balance

Offer Flexibility

Provide flexible working hours and remote work options to help employees balance their personal and professional lives.

Encourage Time Off

Support employees in taking their full vacation time and maintaining boundaries between work and personal life to prevent burnout.

4. Recognize and Reward Achievements

Regular Recognition

Acknowledge individual and team accomplishments regularly. Praise can be given verbally, through emails, or during meetings.

Implement Reward Programs

Establish formal reward systems, such as bonuses, promotions, or employee of the month programs, to motivate and recognize outstanding performance.

5. Foster Team Collaboration

Create Collaborative Spaces

Design work spaces that facilitate teamwork, such as open office layouts and meeting rooms. Use collaboration tools for remote teams.

Encourage Team-Building Activities
    Organize activities that promote bonding and teamwork, such as retreats, workshops, and social events.

6. Support Professional Development

Provide Training Opportunities
    Invest in employee development by offering training programs, workshops, and courses that enhance skills and knowledge.

Create Clear Career Paths
    Offer clear career progression opportunities. Encourage employees to set professional goals and support them in achieving these objectives.

7. Ensure Transparent Communication

Open Communication Channels
    Maintain open lines of communication where employees can freely share ideas, feedback, and concerns.

Regular Updates
    Keep employees informed about company news, changes, and goals through regular updates, meetings, and newsletters.

8. Prioritize Employee Well-being

Health and Wellness Programs
    Implement programs that support physical and mental health, such as gym memberships, wellness workshops, and access to mental health resources.

Create a Supportive Environment

Foster an environment where employees feel valued and supported. Address their needs and concerns with empathy and prompt action.

9. Embrace Diversity and Inclusion

Diverse Hiring Practices
Commit to hiring practices that promote diversity, ensuring a mix of backgrounds, perspectives, and experiences within the organization.

Cultivate an Inclusive Culture
Promote an inclusive culture where every employee feels respected and valued, regardless of their background or role.

10. Celebrate Success and Learn from Failure

Celebrate Milestones
Celebrate both individual and collective achievements. Recognizing successes fosters a sense of accomplishment and unity.

Learn from Mistakes
Encourage a culture where mistakes are seen as opportunities for learning and growth. Analyzing and learning from failures promotes continuous improvement.

Fostering a positive culture requires intentional effort and consistency. By defining and communicating core values, leading by example, promoting work-life balance, recognizing achievements, fostering collaboration, supporting professional development, ensuring transparent communication, prioritizing well-being, embracing diversity and inclusion, and celebrating success while learning from failure, you create an environment where employees feel valued, motivated, and engaged. This not only enhances individual and team performance but also drives the long-term success of your organization.

Empower Your Team

Delegate responsibilities and trust your team members to execute their tasks. Empowering your team fosters a sense of ownership and accountability.

Empowering your team is about giving employees the autonomy, resources, and confidence they need to take initiative, make decisions, and perform their best. Empowered employees feel valued and motivated, which can lead to increased productivity, innovation, and job satisfaction. Here's how to effectively empower your team:

1. Delegate Authority and Responsibility

Trust Your Team

Show trust in your employees by delegating tasks and responsibilities. Allow them to take ownership of projects and make decisions related to their work.

Define Clear Boundaries

While giving autonomy, ensure that the scope of their responsibilities is clearly defined. This helps in avoiding confusion and ensures accountability.

2. Provide the Necessary Resources

Equip with Tools and Training

Ensure that employees have access to the tools, training, and resources they need to perform their tasks effectively. This includes software, hardware, and educational resources.

Support Continuous Learning

Encourage and facilitate continuous learning and development. Offer opportunities for employees to attend workshops, courses, and conferences.

3. Foster a Culture of Open Communication

Encourage Feedback

Create an environment where employees feel comfortable sharing their ideas, feedback, and concerns. Regularly solicit their input on processes, projects, and decisions.

Be Approachable
Maintain an open-door policy. Make yourself accessible to employees for discussions, advice, and support.

4. Recognize and Reward Initiative

Acknowledge Efforts
Recognize and reward employees who take initiative and contribute positively. This could be through verbal praise, awards, or other incentives.

Celebrate Success
Celebrate both individual and team successes. Acknowledging achievements reinforces the value of taking initiative and encourages a proactive attitude.

5. Set Clear Goals and Expectations

Define Objectives
Set clear, achievable goals for your team. Ensure that these goals align with the overall mission and vision of the organization.

Provide Guidance
While giving autonomy, provide necessary guidance and support. Make sure employees understand what is expected of them and how their work contributes to the organization's objectives.

6. Encourage Innovation and Creativity

Promote Experimentation
Encourage employees to experiment with new ideas and approaches. Create

a safe environment where they can take calculated risks without fear of failure.

Value Diverse Perspectives

Foster an inclusive culture that values diverse perspectives and ideas. Encourage collaboration and brainstorming sessions where everyone can contribute.

7. Build Confidence

Offer Constructive Feedback

Provide constructive feedback that helps employees grow and improve. Focus on strengths as well as areas for development.

Mentor and Coach

Act as a mentor and coach. Offer guidance, support, and encouragement to help employees build their skills and confidence.

8. Allow for Flexibility

Flexible Work Arrangements

Offer flexible work arrangements such as remote work, flexible hours, and job-sharing. Flexibility can help employees manage their work-life balance more effectively.

Autonomy in Work

Give employees the freedom to choose how they complete their tasks. Allow them to find the most effective and efficient ways to achieve their goals.

9. Promote Accountability

Set Clear Expectations

Clearly communicate expectations and hold employees accountable for their work. Accountability helps in ensuring that employees take ownership of their responsibilities.

Monitor Progress

Regularly check in on progress and provide support as needed. Ensure that employees have the resources and guidance required to meet their objectives.

10. Provide Support and Resources

Address Challenges

Help employees overcome challenges by providing necessary resources and support. Be proactive in identifying and addressing obstacles that may hinder their performance.

Encourage Collaboration

Foster a collaborative environment where employees can seek help and support from their colleagues. Encourage teamwork and knowledge sharing.

Empowering your team is about creating an environment where employees feel trusted, valued, and capable of making meaningful contributions. By delegating authority, providing necessary resources, fostering open communication, recognizing efforts, setting clear goals, encouraging innovation, building confidence, allowing flexibility, promoting accountability, and offering support, you can cultivate a workforce that is motivated, engaged, and driven to achieve both individual and organizational success. Empowered employees are more likely to take initiative, solve problems, and drive continuous improvement, leading to a more dynamic and successful organization.

Chapter 3

Cultivate Emotional Intelligence

Cultivating emotional intelligence (EI) is essential for creating a supportive, productive, and collaborative workplace. Emotional intelligence involves understanding and managing your own emotions and recognizing and influencing the emotions of others. Here's how to cultivate emotional intelligence within yourself and your team:

1. Develop Self-Awareness

Reflect on Emotions
    Regularly reflect on your own emotions and how they affect your thoughts and actions. Journaling or mindfulness practices can help you become more aware of your emotional responses.

Seek Feedback
    Ask for feedback from colleagues, friends, or mentors to gain insights into how others perceive your emotional responses and behaviors.

2. Practice Self-Regulation

Manage Stress

Develop strategies for managing stress, such as deep breathing exercises, meditation, or physical activity. Staying calm under pressure helps in maintaining control over your emotions.

Stay Composed

Practice staying composed and measured in your responses, especially in challenging situations. Avoid impulsive reactions and take time to respond thoughtfully.

Set Boundaries

Learn to set healthy boundaries to protect your well-being and prevent emotional burnout. This includes saying no when necessary and managing your workload effectively.

3. Improve Social Awareness

Observe Others

Pay attention to the emotional cues of those around you. Observe body language, facial expressions, and tone of voice to better understand their feelings.

Empathy

Practice empathy by putting yourself in others' shoes. Try to understand their perspectives, emotions, and experiences without judgment.

Active Listening

Engage in active listening by fully focusing on the speaker, acknowledging their points, and responding appropriately. This demonstrates respect and understanding.

4. Enhance Relationship Management

Effective Communication

Communicate clearly and respectfully. Use "I" statements to express your feelings and needs without blaming or criticizing others.

Conflict Resolution
Develop skills in resolving conflicts constructively. Focus on finding solutions rather than assigning blame, and strive for win-win outcomes.

Build Trust
Build trust by being consistent, reliable, and transparent. Honesty and integrity are key components of strong, trusting relationships.

5. Encourage Emotional Intelligence in the Workplace

Lead by Example
Model emotionally intelligent behavior in your interactions with others. Your behavior sets a standard for the rest of the team.

Training and Development
Offer training programs and workshops on emotional intelligence. Provide resources and opportunities for employees to develop their EI skills.

Supportive Environment
Create a supportive work environment where employees feel safe expressing their emotions. Encourage open communication and provide resources for emotional support.

6. Foster a Positive Work Environment

Recognition and Praise
Regularly recognize and praise employees for their contributions. Positive reinforcement boosts morale and fosters a sense of belonging.

Encourage Teamwork

Promote collaboration and teamwork. Encourage employees to support each other and work together towards common goals.

Balance Feedback

Provide balanced feedback that includes both positive reinforcement and constructive criticism. Focus on behaviors and outcomes rather than personal attributes.

7. Implement EI Practices in Daily Operations

Mindfulness Practices

Introduce mindfulness practices such as meditation sessions, breathing exercises, or quiet reflection times. These can help employees manage stress and maintain emotional balance.

Emotional Check-Ins

Incorporate emotional check-ins in meetings to gauge the team's emotional state. This can help identify and address any underlying issues early.

Peer Support Groups

Establish peer support groups where employees can share their experiences and offer mutual support. This fosters a sense of community and collective resilience.

8. Measure and Improve EI

Self-Assessment Tools

Use self-assessment tools and surveys to measure emotional intelligence levels among employees. These tools can help identify areas for improvement.

Continuous Improvement

Encourage continuous improvement in EI skills. Regularly review and update training programs and provide ongoing opportunities for development.

Feedback Mechanisms

Implement feedback mechanisms that allow employees to share their experiences and suggestions for improving emotional intelligence initiatives.

Cultivating emotional intelligence within yourself and your team is a continuous process that requires commitment and practice. By developing self-awareness, practicing self-regulation, improving social awareness, enhancing relationship management, and encouraging EI in the workplace, you can create a more empathetic, collaborative, and productive environment. Emotional intelligence not only improves individual well-being but also strengthens team dynamics and drives organizational success. Through ongoing efforts and support, you can foster a workplace culture where emotional intelligence is valued and nurtured.

Chapter 4

Strategic Thinking and Decision Making

Analyze Data

Use data analytics to inform your decisions. Understand key metrics and use them to guide your strategies.

As a CEO, analyzing data involves leveraging information to drive strategic decisions and operational improvements across the organization. Here's a concise overview of how a CEO approaches data analysis:

1. Define Objectives: Clearly outline the strategic goals or specific problems that data analysis aims to address, such as improving operational efficiency, understanding customer behavior, or identifying growth opportunities.

2. Data Collection: Ensure data is collected from relevant sources, both internal (e.g., sales records, customer databases) and external (e.g., market trends, industry reports), to provide a comprehensive view.

3. Quality Assurance: Verify the accuracy, completeness, and reliability of data through validation processes and data cleaning techniques to eliminate errors or inconsistencies.

4. Analysis Methods: Apply appropriate analytical methods, such as statistical

analysis, predictive modeling, or machine learning algorithms, to extract insights and patterns from the data.

5. Interpretation: Interpret the analyzed data to extract actionable insights and strategic implications. This involves understanding trends, correlations, and potential causal relationships within the data.

6. Decision Making: Utilize insights gained from data analysis to inform decision-making processes. This may involve strategic planning, resource allocation, product development, marketing strategies, or operational improvements.

7. Monitoring and Optimization: Continuously monitor key performance indicators (KPIs) and metrics derived from data analysis to track progress, evaluate outcomes, and adjust strategies as needed for ongoing optimization.

8. Communication: Effectively communicate findings and recommendations derived from data analysis to stakeholders, such as executive team members, board of directors, or department heads, to foster alignment and support for strategic initiatives.

By effectively analyzing data, CEOs can gain a deeper understanding of market dynamics, customer preferences, operational efficiencies, and competitive landscapes, enabling them to make informed decisions that drive organizational success and sustainable growth.

Risk Management

Identify potential risks and develop mitigation plans. Be prepared to adapt and respond to unforeseen challenges.

As a CEO, risk management involves identifying, assessing, and mitigating potential risks that could impact the organization's objectives and operations. Here's a concise overview of how a CEO approaches risk management:

1. Risk Identification: Identify and categorize risks that could affect the organization, including strategic, financial, operational, compliance, and reputational risks.

2. Risk Assessment: Evaluate the likelihood and potential impact of identified risks using qualitative or quantitative methods. Prioritize risks based on their significance and potential consequences.

3. Risk Mitigation: Develop and implement strategies and controls to mitigate or reduce identified risks to an acceptable level. This may include implementing internal controls, enhancing security measures, diversifying risks, or purchasing insurance.

4. Monitoring and Review: Continuously monitor and review risk factors and mitigation strategies. Regularly assess changes in the internal and external environment that may affect risk levels.

5. Risk Communication: Communicate risk management strategies, policies, and outcomes to stakeholders, including board members, senior executives, employees, and external partners. Foster a culture of risk awareness and responsibility throughout the organization.

6. Integration with Strategic Planning: Integrate risk management into strategic planning processes to ensure alignment with organizational goals and objectives. Consider risks and opportunities when making strategic decisions.

7. Adaptability and Resilience: Build organizational resilience by anticipating potential risks, adapting to changing circumstances, and responding effectively to crises or unexpected events.

By effectively managing risks, CEOs can enhance organizational resilience, protect assets and reputation, foster stakeholder confidence, and ensure sustainable long-term success.

Innovation

Encourage a culture of innovation. Stay open to new ideas and be willing to invest in research and development.

As a CEO, fostering innovation involves creating an environment where new ideas, processes, products, or services can thrive to drive business growth and competitive advantage. Here's a concise overview of how a CEO approaches innovation:

1. Encourage a Culture of Innovation: Cultivate a work environment that values creativity, experimentation, and continuous improvement. Encourage employees at all levels to contribute ideas and take calculated risks.

2. Set Strategic Objectives: Define clear strategic objectives for innovation aligned with the organization's vision and goals. These objectives should guide innovation efforts and prioritize areas for investment and development.

3. Allocate Resources: Allocate sufficient resources, including funding, time, and talent, to support innovation initiatives. Invest in research and development, technology, and training programs that foster innovation.

4. Promote Collaboration: Encourage cross-functional collaboration and teamwork to generate diverse perspectives and ideas. Create opportunities for employees, departments, and external partners to collaborate on innovation projects.

5. Embrace Technology and Trends: Stay abreast of industry trends, technological advancements, and market changes that present opportunities for innovation. Leverage emerging technologies and digital transformation to drive innovation.

6. Support Risk-Taking: Foster a culture where calculated risks are encour-

aged and failure is viewed as a learning opportunity. Provide support and resources for innovative projects, even if outcomes are uncertain.

7. Customer-Centric Approach: Maintain a deep understanding of customer needs, preferences, and pain points. Use customer insights to inform innovation strategies and develop solutions that deliver value and differentiation.

8. Measure and Evaluate: Establish metrics and KPIs to measure the success and impact of innovation initiatives. Regularly evaluate progress against goals and adjust strategies as needed to optimize outcomes.

9. Lead by Example: Demonstrate leadership in fostering innovation by championing new ideas, supporting innovators, and celebrating successful innovations. Set an example of openness to change and continuous improvement.

10. Strategic Partnerships: Form strategic partnerships with startups, universities, research institutions, and industry leaders to access external expertise, technologies, and innovation ecosystems.

By prioritizing and nurturing innovation, CEOs can drive organizational growth, enhance competitiveness, and create sustainable value for customers, employees, and stakeholders alike.

Chapter 5

Financial Acumen

Financial acumen is essential for a CEO to make informed decisions that drive the organization's success. Here's how to develop and leverage financial acumen to be the best CEO ever:

1. Understand Financial Statements:
   - Gain a deep understanding of key financial statements—balance sheets, income statements, and cash flow statements. This knowledge helps in assessing the company's financial health.

2. Budgeting and Forecasting:
   - Master the principles of budgeting and financial forecasting. Accurate budgeting and forecasting are crucial for planning, resource allocation, and anticipating future financial needs.

   Manage the company's finances prudently. Ensure that budgets align with strategic goals and are adhered to.

   Budgeting is a critical aspect of a CEO's role, as it ensures the organization's resources are allocated efficiently to achieve strategic goals.

3. Analyze Key Metrics:
   - Track and analyze critical financial metrics such as revenue growth, profit margins, return on investment (ROI), and earnings before interest, taxes,

depreciation, and amortization (EBITDA).

4. Cost Management:

   - Implement effective cost management strategies to control expenses without compromising quality or innovation. Understand cost structures and identify areas for efficiency improvements.

   Optimize operations to reduce costs without compromising quality or employee satisfaction.

5. Investment Decisions:

   - Evaluate potential investments thoroughly. Assess risks, returns, and strategic alignment. Make decisions that enhance the company's value and growth prospects.

   Make informed decisions about investments. Balance short-term needs with long-term growth opportunities.

6. Risk Management:

   - Identify financial risks and develop strategies to mitigate them. This includes managing debt levels, maintaining cash reserves, and diversifying revenue streams.

7. Leverage Financial Tools:

   - Use financial management tools and software for real-time tracking, analysis, and reporting. These tools can enhance decision-making accuracy and efficiency.

8. Stay Informed:

   - Keep up-to-date with financial news, market trends, and regulatory changes. This knowledge helps in anticipating challenges and seizing opportunities.

9. Communicate Financial Insights:

   - Clearly communicate financial performance and strategies to stakeholders, including the board, investors, and employees. Transparency builds trust and aligns everyone with the company's financial goals.

10. Continuous Learning:

   - Invest in continuous learning to enhance financial skills. Attend workshops, courses, or seminars on financial management and stay current with industry best practices.

11. Collaborate with Financial Experts:

   - Work closely with your CFO and financial team. Their expertise can provide valuable insights and support in making sound financial decisions.

By cultivating financial acumen, a CEO can effectively manage the company's resources, drive profitability, and ensure long-term financial stability and growth.

Chapter 6

Build Strong Relationships

1. Communicate Effectively:
   - Practice clear, open, and honest communication. Regularly update stakeholders about company goals, challenges, and successes to build transparency and trust.

2. Listen Actively:
   - Show genuine interest in others' perspectives and concerns. Active listening demonstrates respect and helps in understanding the needs and motivations of employees, customers, and partners.

3. Empathy and Emotional Intelligence:
   - Display empathy and emotional intelligence in interactions. Understanding and addressing the emotions and concerns of others fosters deeper connections and loyalty.

4. Engage with Employees:
   - Be approachable and visible within the organization. Engage with employees at all levels, showing appreciation for their contributions and encouraging a sense of belonging.

5. Network Strategically:

- Build a robust professional network by connecting with industry leaders, peers, and potential partners. Networking opens opportunities for collaborations, partnerships, and valuable insights.

Establish and nurture relationships with industry leaders, partners, and potential clients. Networking can open doors to new opportunities and collaborations.

Building strong relationships is crucial for a CEO to foster collaboration, trust, and loyalty within and outside the organization. Here's how to build and maintain strong relationships to be the best CEO ever:

6. Mentorship and Support:

- Act as a mentor and support system for employees. Provide guidance, encourage professional growth, and recognize their achievements, which helps in building strong, motivated teams.

7. Customer Relationships:

- Prioritize building strong relationships with customers. Understand their needs, deliver exceptional value, and maintain regular communication to foster loyalty and long-term partnerships.

Prioritize customer satisfaction. Understand their needs and continuously improve your products or services to meet these demands.

8. Collaborate with Stakeholders:

- Develop strong relationships with key stakeholders, including investors, board members, and suppliers. Align their interests with the company's goals through consistent and transparent communication.

Maintain transparent and consistent communication with all stakeholders. Build trust through reliability and integrity.

9. Community Engagement:

- Engage with the community and industry. Participate in community events, industry forums, and social responsibility initiatives to build a positive reputation and strengthen external relationships.

10. Lead by Example:
   - Demonstrate integrity, reliability, and respect in all interactions. Leading by example sets the standard for behavior within the organization and earns the trust and respect of others.

11. Conflict Resolution:
   - Address conflicts promptly and fairly. Effective conflict resolution helps maintain positive relationships and a healthy organizational culture.

12. Feedback and Improvement:
   - Seek and provide constructive feedback. Encourage an environment where feedback is valued and used for continuous improvement and relationship building.

By focusing on building strong relationships, a CEO can create a cohesive and motivated organization, foster loyalty and trust among stakeholders, and enhance the company's reputation and success.

Chapter 7

Adaptability and Resilience

Adaptability and resilience are essential traits for a CEO to navigate challenges and drive the organization towards sustained success. Here's how to develop and demonstrate these qualities to be the best CEO:

Adaptability

1. Embrace Change:
   - Be open to change and encourage a culture that views change as an opportunity rather than a threat. Adapt quickly to new information, technologies, and market conditions.

2. Continuous Learning:
   - Commit to lifelong learning. Stay updated with industry trends, emerging technologies, and best practices. Encourage your team to do the same.

3. Flexible Thinking:
   - Develop flexible thinking by considering multiple perspectives and solutions. Be willing to pivot strategies and approaches when necessary.

4. Encourage Innovation:

- Foster an innovative environment where creative ideas are valued and explored. Support experimentation and be open to new ways of doing things.

5. Empower Teams:
   - Delegate authority and empower teams to make decisions. Encourage them to adapt their approaches based on real-time feedback and changing circumstances.

6. Scenario Planning:
   - Engage in scenario planning to anticipate potential changes and prepare for various future scenarios. This proactive approach helps in responding effectively to unexpected developments.

Resilience

1. Stay Positive:
   - Maintain a positive attitude, especially during tough times. Your optimism can inspire and motivate the team to overcome challenges.

2. Develop Coping Strategies:
   - Implement coping strategies to manage stress and maintain mental and emotional well-being. Encourage the same for your team.

3. Focus on Core Values:
   - Stay grounded in the organization's core values and mission. This provides a stable foundation during turbulent times.

4. Build a Support Network:
   - Cultivate a strong support network of mentors, peers, and advisors. Seek their advice and support when facing challenges.

5. Learn from Failures:
   - View failures and setbacks as learning opportunities. Analyze what went

wrong, extract lessons, and use them to improve future performance.

6. Maintain Financial Health:
   - Ensure the organization has a strong financial foundation. Build reserves and manage cash flow effectively to withstand economic downturns and unexpected expenses.

7. Communicate Transparently:
   - Communicate openly and honestly with your team and stakeholders during crises. Transparency builds trust and helps everyone stay aligned and focused.

8. Focus on Long-Term Goals:
   - Keep sight of long-term goals and vision, even when addressing short-term challenges. This long-term focus helps maintain direction and purpose.

Implementing Adaptability and Resilience

- Training and Development: Invest in training programs that enhance adaptability and resilience skills across the organization. This builds a more agile and robust workforce.

- Feedback Loops: Establish feedback loops to continuously learn and adapt from experiences. Regularly review performance and make necessary adjustments.

- Celebrate Successes: Acknowledge and celebrate successes, no matter how small, to boost morale and reinforce positive behavior.

By embodying adaptability and resilience, a CEO can effectively lead the organization through change and adversity, ensuring long-term stability and success.

Chapter 8

Lead with Integrity

Leading with integrity is fundamental to being an effective and respected CEO. It involves adhering to strong ethical principles, being transparent, and building trust within and outside the organization. Here's how to lead with integrity to be the best CEO ever:

Define and Uphold Ethical Standards
   1. Establish Clear Values:
   - Define and communicate the company's core values and ethical standards. Ensure that these principles guide all decisions and actions.

2. Lead by Example:
   - Demonstrate integrity through your actions. Be consistent in practicing the values you preach, setting a standard for others to follow.

Foster a Culture of Integrity
   3. Create a Transparent Environment:
   - Encourage openness and honesty throughout the organization. Ensure that employees feel comfortable reporting unethical behavior without fear of retaliation.

4. Implement Ethical Policies:

- Develop and enforce policies that promote ethical behavior, such as codes of conduct, conflict of interest guidelines, and anti-corruption measures.

Decision-Making with Integrity

5. Prioritize Ethical Decision-Making:

- Make decisions that align with the company's ethical standards, even when they might be difficult or less profitable in the short term. Consider the long-term impact on stakeholders.

6. Transparency and Accountability:

- Be transparent about decisions and their rationale. Hold yourself and others accountable for actions and outcomes, admitting mistakes and taking corrective action when necessary.

Build Trust and Credibility

7. Communicate Honestly:

- Communicate openly with employees, customers, investors, and other stakeholders. Provide truthful information, even when it's challenging.

8. Respect Confidentiality:

- Protect sensitive information and respect the privacy of employees and customers. This builds trust and confidence in your leadership.

Develop Ethical Leadership

9. Invest in Training:

- Provide regular training on ethical behavior and decision-making for all employees. Reinforce the importance of integrity in all aspects of the business.

10. Reward Integrity:

- Recognize and reward employees who demonstrate ethical behavior and uphold company values. This reinforces the importance of integrity within the organization.

Engage with Stakeholders

11. Build Honest Relationships:

- Cultivate relationships based on honesty and mutual respect with all stakeholders, including customers, suppliers, and the community.

12. Commit to Corporate Social Responsibility (CSR):

- Actively engage in CSR initiatives that reflect the company's values and commitment to making a positive impact on society.

Long-Term Perspective

13. Sustainable Practices:

- Implement sustainable business practices that consider the well-being of the environment and society. Ethical leadership ensures the company's long-term success and reputation.

14. Ethical Risk Management:

- Identify and mitigate ethical risks. Regularly review and update policies to address emerging ethical challenges and ensure compliance with laws and regulations.

Conclusion

Leading with integrity as a CEO means consistently upholding ethical standards, fostering a transparent and accountable culture, and building trust with stakeholders. This approach not only strengthens the company's reputation and relationships but also ensures sustainable success and resilience in the face of challenges. By prioritizing integrity, a CEO can inspire confidence, loyalty, and respect, laying a solid foundation for long-term organizational growth and stability.

Chapter 9

BE AN ENTREPRENEUR

Becoming an entrepreneur involves identifying opportunities, taking risks, and managing a business to achieve growth and success. Here's a step-by-step guide to help you embark on your entrepreneurial journey:

1. Self-Assessment
   - Evaluate Your Skills and Interests: Understand your strengths, weaknesses, passions, and expertise. Successful entrepreneurship often aligns with personal interests and skills.
   - Assess Risk Tolerance: Be prepared for uncertainty and challenges. Consider whether you are comfortable taking calculated risks.

2. Idea Generation
   - Identify Opportunities: Look for gaps in the market, problems that need solving, or areas where you can offer better solutions than existing ones.
   - Brainstorm Ideas: Think creatively and brainstorm multiple business ideas. Consider how each idea aligns with market needs and your personal strengths.

3. Research and Validation
   - Conduct Market Research: Analyze the market to understand demand,

competition, and potential customers. Validate your idea with real-world data.

   - Seek Feedback: Share your idea with potential customers, mentors, and industry experts to gather feedback and refine your concept.

4. Business Planning

   - Develop a Business Plan: Create a detailed business plan outlining your business model, target market, value proposition, revenue streams, marketing strategy, and financial projections.

   - Set Goals: Define short-term and long-term goals. Establish clear milestones to measure progress.

5. Funding

   - Determine Funding Needs: Calculate the startup costs and operating expenses required to launch and sustain your business.

   - Explore Funding Options: Consider various funding sources, such as personal savings, loans, investors, crowdfunding, or grants.

6. Legal and Administrative Setup

   - Choose a Business Structure: Decide on the legal structure of your business (e.g., sole proprietorship, partnership, LLC, corporation) based on your needs and goals.

   - Register Your Business: Register your business name and obtain necessary licenses and permits. Ensure compliance with local, state, and federal regulations.

7. Build Your Brand

   - Create a Brand Identity: Develop a strong brand identity, including a logo, tagline, and brand values. Ensure consistency across all marketing materials.

   - Develop an Online Presence: Build a professional website and establish a presence on social media platforms relevant to your audience.

8. Launch and Marketing

- Plan Your Launch: Develop a launch strategy to introduce your business to the market. Consider promotional activities, events, or campaigns.

- Implement Marketing Strategies: Use a mix of marketing tactics (e.g., content marketing, social media, email marketing, SEO) to reach your target audience and generate sales.

9. Operations and Management

-Set Up Operations: Establish efficient processes and systems for daily operations. This includes supply chain management, inventory control, and customer service.

- Hire and Manage Team: If needed, recruit and manage a team. Foster a positive work culture and provide ongoing training and support.

10. Monitor and Adapt

- Track Performance: Regularly review business performance using key metrics and KPIs. Assess financial health, customer satisfaction, and operational efficiency.

- Adapt and Innovate: Stay flexible and open to change. Continuously seek ways to improve products, services, and processes based on feedback and market trends.

11. Networking and Growth

- Network with Other Entrepreneurs: Join industry associations, attend events, and connect with other entrepreneurs to share experiences and gain insights.

- Scale Your Business: Plan for growth by exploring new markets, expanding product lines, or enhancing your offerings. Invest in scalable systems and technologies.

12. Persistence and Resilience

- Stay Committed: Be prepared for setbacks and challenges. Persistence and resilience are key to overcoming obstacles and achieving long-term success.

- Learn Continuously: Keep learning and evolving. Stay informed about industry trends, new technologies, and best practices to maintain a competitive edge.

By following these steps, you can navigate the journey of entrepreneurship with confidence and increase your chances of building a successful and sustainable business.

Chapter 10

10 Stories of Successful Entrepreneurs

Here are some success stories of entrepreneurs who have made a significant impact through their innovative ideas, perseverance, and leadership:

1. Steve Jobs - Apple Inc.

Steve Jobs co-founded Apple Inc. in 1976, starting in a garage with Steve Wozniak and Ronald Wayne. Despite facing numerous setbacks, including being ousted from his own company in 1985, Jobs' vision and relentless pursuit of innovation led to the creation of iconic products like the iPhone, iPad, and MacBook. His return to Apple in 1997 marked a turning point, leading the company to become one of the most valuable brands in the world.

2. Elon Musk - Tesla and SpaceX

Elon Musk is a serial entrepreneur known for his ambitious ventures. He founded Zip2 and X.com (which became PayPal), before moving on to Tesla Motors and SpaceX. Despite early skepticism and numerous challenges, Musk's vision for sustainable energy and space exploration has revolutionized industries. Tesla has become a leader in electric vehicles, while SpaceX has achieved milestones like reusable rockets and plans for Mars colonization.

3. Oprah Winfrey - Harpo Productions

Oprah Winfrey overcame a challenging childhood to become one of the most influential media moguls. Starting as a television news anchor, she eventually launched "The Oprah Winfrey Show," which became the highest-rated talk show in history. Winfrey later founded Harpo Productions, her own production company, and launched the Oprah Winfrey Network (OWN). Her influence extends beyond media, with impactful contributions to philanthropy and social causes.

4. Sara Blakely - Spanx

Sara Blakely founded Spanx with just $5,000 in savings and a brilliant idea for women's shapewear. She faced numerous rejections before Neiman Marcus agreed to carry her products. Blakely's perseverance and innovative marketing strategies turned Spanx into a billion-dollar business, revolutionizing the undergarment industry. She became the youngest self-made female billionaire in America.

5. Jeff Bezos - Amazon

Jeff Bezos started Amazon in 1994 as an online bookstore. Despite initial skepticism and financial struggles, Bezos' long-term vision and relentless focus on customer experience led Amazon to become the world's largest online retailer. Bezos expanded the company into various sectors, including cloud computing (AWS), entertainment (Amazon Prime), and artificial intelligence, making Amazon a global powerhouse.

6. Richard Branson - Virgin Group

Richard Branson founded Virgin Records in 1972, which grew into a major label. He expanded the Virgin brand into various industries, including airlines (Virgin Atlantic), telecommunications (Virgin Mobile), and space travel (Virgin Galactic). Known for his adventurous spirit and innovative approach, Branson built the Virgin Group into a global conglomerate with over 400 companies.

7. Jan Koum - WhatsApp

Jan Koum, born in Ukraine, immigrated to the U.S. and faced financial hardships. He co-founded WhatsApp in 2009, focusing on creating a simple, ad-free messaging app. The app gained massive popularity due to its user-friendly design and privacy features. In 2014, Facebook acquired WhatsApp for $19 billion, making Koum a billionaire and cementing WhatsApp's place as one of the most popular messaging platforms globally.

8. Howard Schultz - Starbucks

Howard Schultz joined Starbucks in 1982 and transformed it from a small coffee bean retailer into a global coffeehouse chain. Schultz's vision of creating a "third place" between home and work resonated with customers, leading to rapid expansion and international success. Under his leadership, Starbucks became synonymous with premium coffee and a unique customer experience.

9. Melanie Perkins - Canva

Melanie Perkins co-founded Canva in 2012 with the goal of democratizing design. Despite facing initial rejections from investors, Canva's intuitive online design platform quickly gained traction. Perkins' vision and persistence paid off as Canva grew into a multi-billion dollar company, empowering millions of users worldwide to create professional-quality designs easily.

10. Jack Ma - Alibaba Group

Jack Ma, a former English teacher, founded Alibaba Group in 1999 to connect Chinese manufacturers with international buyers. Despite limited resources and early struggles, Ma's determination and innovative approach turned Alibaba into a global e-commerce giant. Today, Alibaba encompasses various businesses, including online marketplaces, cloud computing, and digital entertainment, making Ma one of China's richest individuals.

These 10 stories highlight the diverse paths to entrepreneurial success, showcasing the importance of vision, resilience, and innovation in achieving greatness.

Conclusion

Becoming the best CEO ever is a continuous journey of growth and improvement. It requires a combination of strategic vision, strong leadership, emotional intelligence, financial savvy, and unwavering integrity. By following these guidelines and consistently striving to improve, you can lead your organization to unparalleled success and make a lasting impact in your industry.